Full Employment at Any Price?

F. A. HAYEK

Nobel Laureate 1974

Published by

THE INSTITUTE OF ECONOMIC AFFAIRS
1975

First published July 1975

by

THE INSTITUTE OF ECONOMIC AFFAIRS

SBN 255 36070-3

Printed in Great Britain by
TONBRIDGE PRINTERS LTD, TONBRIDGE KENT
Set in Monotype Plantin

Contents

[4]

Preface

THE *Occasional Papers* were created primarily to make available to a wider audience essays or addresses directed at specialist assemblies.

About the wider interest in the three lectures assembled here there can be no question. Part I comprises a lecture on the causation of unemployment delivered to an academic audience in Italy. Part II is the Alfred Nobel Memorial Lecture on the methodology of economics, which may seem more remote from immediate concern but goes to the root of the social sciences, and bears directly on the debate among economists on the causation of unemployment. Part III adds refinements of the argument and analysis. None of the material has been published previously.

In Part I Professor Hayek has created a microcosm both of the economic and monetary history of half a century since the 1920s and also of his economic thinking, in particular his differences from the trend of economic thought fathered by J. M. Keynes. After 45 years since he first crossed swords with Keynes in 1931, Professor Hayek maintains that the Keynesian diagnosis, developed in *The General Theory of Employment, Interest and Money* of 1936, was fallacious and that, although there seem to have been several decades of high or full employment, the fallacy is now being revealed. He maintains that the cause of unemployment is not inadequate demand arising from inadequate total income but disproportions in *relative* wages required to equate the demand for labour and its supply in each sector of the economy. He maintains, *first*, that it is now becoming clear that inflation can absorb unemployment only for a period but makes it worse and inevitable in the longer run, and *second*, that the inflation is not a once-for-all but a continuing and accelerating process that can end by destroying the currency, monetary institutions and ultimately society.

Inflation is therefore not the solution for unemployment; nor is it the way to ensure full employment. These truths might have been seen earlier if the war and its long aftermath had not followed so closely on *The General Theory* and if Keynes' recommendations had been applied in the late 1930s or the early 1940s, when the consequences in inflation, industrial distortion and dislocation might have emerged soon enough for their causes in Keynesian policies to be evident. History ordained otherwise.

Professor Hayek says that Keynes would not have approved of the policies pursued after him in his name. But if 'demand management' has now been seen to have failed, other policies must be devised. If the solution must be to remove the misdirection of labour accompanying inflation by re-structuring the system of relative wages, the question for policy-makers is how to provide for more flexibility of the prices of labour and how to make labour markets work more effectively. In the 1930s the argument for inflation to reduce real wages was that money wages were not flexible downwards, i.e. that wage reductions were 'politically impossible'. Professor Hayek now argues that there is no other way to full employment, but says he does not see how, or how soon, it can be achieved. But since policies based on the assumption that flexibility is 'politically impossible' do not provide alternatives that operate in the long run or that are compatible with a free society, the only way is by revision of long-established resistances to change in consumer demand or technology and reform of long-established laws governing collective bargaining and the labour market.

Although Professor Hayek says he would not predict what chances there are of ensuring that relative wage-rates are determined by 'market forces' so that the demand for and the supply of labour are equated, he suggests how the *impasse* of 1975 should be handled. He would stop the increase in the supply of money, or at least reduce it to the real rate of growth in output; and he would do it immediately, not gradually. He would prevent a deflation in *absolute* incomes. And, by announcing the intention, prevent the recession from degenerating into a depression. But in the long run the solution would have to be a re-structuring of the wages system.

In spite therefore of some differences with the 'monetarists', Professor Hayek is arguing essentially for policy to reform the labour markets on the ground that monetary policy alone cannot remove unemployment. And it is here perhaps that economic analysis should now increasingly concentrate.

How is it that the economic theory that has held the stage for so long was widely accepted among economists and even more widely among politicians soon after it was publicised by Keynes? Professor Hayek maintains in his Nobel Memorial Lecture that the reason is basically that the supposed link between total demand and total employment seemed to be confirmed by statistical evidence and it was therefore accepted as the only important *causal* connection. In contrast the theory he held in the 1930s, and still maintains is the correct explanation of unemployment, could not be supported by statistical evidence. The false theory was accepted because there was apparent supporting evidence accepted as 'scientific'.

This is the fallacy of 'scientism' which has led to the 'pretence of knowledge' that Professor Hayek makes the subject and title of his Nobel Lecture. Although it thus appears to be mainly of methodological interest for economists, it offers an intriguing explanation of the reason why economists, governments, civil servants and the world in general have been misled for 40 years. The 'scientistic' error is to suppose that the methods of the physical sciences, where causes are normally measurable, can be shifted to the social sciences, where the 'essentially complex' phenomena arising from very large numbers of causes are rarely observable or measurable directly. Economists have therefore been led to the 'fiction' that only measurable factors are relevant. Such a (macro-economic) 'fiction' is the alleged dependence of (total) employment on total demand, without reference to (micro-economic) changes in relative wages. And Professor Hayek is strongly critical of the general misuse of macro-methods and mathematics, which refuse to recognise that, while we can explain general patterns of development, we cannot in the social sciences determine or predict numerical values of individual events.

In his contribution to the IEA seminar on inflation in September 1974 Mr Peter Jay, Economics Editor of *The Times*, identified four types of economic thinking on the role of the trade unions in the causation of inflation: the Marxist, the Keynesian, the Friedmanite, and the Hayekian. The Marxist interpretation of economic history has not lacked interpreters and popularisers, and has been developed in recent years in the economics faculty of the University of Cambridge. The Keynesian approach dominated economic thinking in Britain for 40 years. The Friedmanite

[7]

school, although it has made inroads into the prevailing Keynesian climate and is influential in North America and other continents, was not widely understood in Britain until recently, when the Institute began to make it better known.[1] Although Professor Hayek taught at the London School of Economics from 1931 to 1950, his economic theories are now rarely discussed in Britain. Yet they have a distinguished ancestry in the Austrian School of Carl Menger (1840–1921), Friedrich von Wieser (1851–1926), Eugen von Böhm-Bawerk (1851–1914) and Ludwig von Mises (1881–1973),[2] which has created a distinctive contribution to economic thinking in its emphasis on the structure of production and the inter-related movements in the prices and outputs of capital, intermediate and consumption goods. Here the Keynesian (and subsequent) macro-emphasis on *average* prices and *total* output and employment in the economy as a whole seems to have tacitly assumed more flexibility in prices and more mobility in labour between the stages of production than it allows for in judging the performance of micro-markets.

The series of extracts from Professor Hayek's writings over the last 45 years in *A Tiger by the Tail* attracted wide attention when it was published in 1972. *The Times*[3] recently singled him out as providing the 'explicit framework of analysis within which the nature of the troubles [of inflation and unemployment] can be explained and a comprehensive approach to them developed'. The material reproduced here will further remind readers of the Hayekian/'Austrian' approach to economics, and in a dramatic way by showing how it can shed light on our present economic discontents.[4]

[1] Milton Friedman, *The Counter-Revolution in Monetary Theory*, Occasional Paper 33, 1970; *Monetary Correction*, Occasional Paper 41, 1974; *Inflation: Causes, Consequences, Cures*, IEA Readings No. 14, 1974; *Unemployment versus Inflation?*, Occasional Paper 44, 1975.

[2] J. A. Schumpeter (1883–1950) belonged to the Austrian School wholly by origin, although he diverged somewhat in doctrine. A contemporary member who has applied 'Austrian' analysis in writings on capital theory is Professor L. M. Lachmann, who wrote Hobart Paper 56, *Macro-economic Thinking and the Market Economy*, 1973, for the IEA.

[3] 4 January, 1975.

[4] Earlier IEA works on or by Professor Hayek are A. Seldon (ed.), *Agenda for a Free Society*, 1961; *The Confusion of Language in Political Thought*, 1968; *Verdict on Rent Control*, 1972; Sudha Shenoy (compiler), *A Tiger by the Tail*, 1972; *Economic Freedom and Representative Government*, 1973.

Although Professor Hayek now lives in his native Austria he has honoured Britain, by remaining a British citizen, more than she has recognised his contribution to economics and the social sciences. If the Marxist solution for inflation and unemployment by tight centralisation of state control over economic life is rejected, and the Keynesian solution of 'demand management' has been found invalid, increasing attention will be given to the Friedmanite and Hayekian explanations and implications for policy. Although there are analytical differences between them, chiefly whether 'the cause' of inflation is monetary or institutional, both approaches offer enlightenment not available elsewhere.

It is arguable whether the difference in the meaning of 'cause' is real or verbal. At the Seminar on inflation Lord Robbins and Mr Jay thought the difference was semantic; Professors Friedman and David Laidler argued it was real. To elucidate the difference Professor Friedman distinguished between the money supply as the 'proximate cause' and explanations for the increase in the money supply (such as an increase in union power) as the 'deeper causes', and insisted there was a real difference of view arising from the distinction between the analytical and practical aspects. The main difference revolves around the role of trade unions; the Friedmanites argue inflation has been experienced at times and in countries where unions have been weak, so that they cannot be 'the cause'. On the other hand, the true 'test' of the hypothesis may be to compare a country in which unions are strong with the circumstances that would have been experienced if they had been weak, not to compare two countries in the same period, so that the other influences on inflation may be different, or one country at different periods, so that the influences on inflation may have changed.

At a late stage Professor Hayek added Part III, comprising refinements of aspects of the argument. A sub-title in this Part includes the words 'Over-eating and Indigestion' which he uses to describe one of these refinements, and perhaps the most fundamental: that inflation *must* in the end produce unemployment just as over-eating must produce indigestion. An IEA collection of extracts from Professor Hayek's writings was entitled, and became widely known as, *A Tiger by the Tail*. It may be that the general argument of this *Paper* will be referred to as 'Over-eating and

Indigestion', which dramatises its central theme.

Part III also shows the clarity and consistency of Professor Hayek's thinking and conveys a sense of penetration to essentials after decades of study and reflection. Here there is a further illustration of the difference between Keynesian and Austrian explanations of investment. Throughout his life Professor Hayek, as a true scholar, has been more concerned with the truth than with winning the debate, and he has sometimes been thought to be more reticent than he might have been in his judgement of economists from whom he differed and who had attacked him, sometimes bitterly. In a tribute to him Professor Sir Arnold Plant has said:

> 'Those whose advocacy of social change is powered by strong emotion have often been repelled by the cold-blooded nature of his purely intellectual approach. They would do well to reflect that they would not wish a surgeon to operate upon them while his hands were trembling with emotion.'[1]

In Part III (and in one or two places in Part I) Professor Hayek has allowed himself to use graphic and even forceful language about the errors of economists who, he argues, have misled governments since the 1930s by encouraging them to believe they could simultaneously maintain full employment, stable prices and rising living standards by inflationary 'management' of aggregate demand.

The Hayekian theory of unemployment, and the conclusion that inflation is not the way to remove it, will be given more hearing as other explanations that have dominated economic thinking are found to have failed. The Institute now publishes Professor Hayek's three lectures in the belief that their argument will be found of increasing interest to economists and their implications for policy of increasing relevance for governments. The Institute's constitution requires it to dissociate its Trustees, Directors and Advisers from the analysis and conclusions of its authors, but it is glad to present the thinking of a scholar whom history will judge as perhaps the most profound economic philosopher of his time.

May 1975   ARTHUR SELDON

[1] *Selected Economic Essays & Addresses*, Routledge & Kegan Paul for the Institute of Economic Affairs, 1974.

Author's Introduction

THE PRESENT unemployment is the direct result of the short-sighted 'full employment policies' we have been pursuing during the last 25 years. This is the sad truth we must grasp if we are not to be led into measures that would make matters only worse. The sooner we can tear ourselves out of the fool's paradise in which we have been living the better will be the chance that we can keep the period of suffering short.

Nothing is easier than for a time to create additional employment by drawing workers into activities made temporarily attractive by spending upon them additional money created for the purpose. What we have done during the past 25 years was indeed to resort deliberately and systematically to the quick provision of employment precisely by an increase of the monetary circulation which during the preceding 200 years had been brought about regularly by a defect of the credit system and thus became the cause of recurrent depressions.

We should not be surprised at this result after we have successively removed all the barriers that in the past had been erected as defences against the ever-present popular pressure for 'cheap money'. As had happened at the beginning of the period of modern finance we have again been seduced by another silver-tongued persuader into trying another inflationary bubble. And that bubble has now burst. We shall have to pay for that new attempt at a painless quick acquisition of riches by the discovery that much of the artificially-induced 'growth' was a waste of resources and that in harsh truth Britain is living beyond its means.

Urgent as is the need to re-integrate the workless into the productive process, if we are to prevent similar calamities in the future it is no less important that we avoid making matters worse by repeating the mistakes we have made in the recent past. The habits of thought acquired during that generation have unfortunately rendered us susceptible to this weakness. It is to this most urgent task of rethinking the theoretical conceptions that have guided us that the lectures here printed are addressed.

The first two lectures were delivered during the last few months to academic audiences in Sweden and Italy and will appear in due course in the memoirs of the foreign learned institutions to which they were presented. The third, added when the first two were already set up in type, contains elaborations and elucidations I found necessary to add when, during a visit to the United States, I lectured at various places essentially on the lines of the first. I am very grateful to the Institute of Economic Affairs for making them more readily available to British readers by including them in their series of *Occasional Papers*.

April 1975   F. A. HAYEK

The Author

FRIEDRICH AUGUST HAYEK, Dr Jur, Dr Sc Pol (Vienna), DcS (Econ.) (London), Visiting Professor at the University of Salzburg, Austria 1970–74. Educated at the University of Vienna, Director of the Austrian Institute for Economic Research, 1927–31, and Lecturer in Economics at University of Vienna, 1929–31. 1931–50 Tooke Professor of Economic Science and Statistics, University of London. 1950–62 Professor of Social and Moral Science, University of Chicago. Professor of Economics, University of Freiburg i.Brg., West Germany, 1962–68. He was awarded the Alfred Nobel Memorial Prize in Economic Sciences in 1974.

Professor Hayek's most important publications include *Monetary Theory and the Trade Cycle* (1933), *The Pure Theory of Capital* (1941), *The Road to Serfdom* (1944), *Individualism and Economic Order* (1948), *The Counter-Revolution of Science* (1952), and *The Constitution of Liberty* (1960). His latest works are collections of his writings under the titles *Studies in Philosophy, Politics and Economics* (1967) and *Law, Legislation and Liberty* (Vol. I, 1973). He has also edited several books and has published articles in the *Economic Journal, Economica* and other journals. The IEA has published his *The Confusion of Language in Political Thought* (Occasional Paper 20, 1968), his Wincott Memorial Lecture, *Economic Freedom and Representative Government* (Occasional Paper 39, 1973), a collection of his writings with a new essay (assembled by Sudha Shenoy), *A Tiger by the Tail* (Hobart Paperback 4, 1972), and an essay in *Verdict on Rent Control* (IEA Readings No. 7, 1972).

PART I

*Inflation, the Misdirection of Labour, and Unemployment**

I
INFLATION AND UNEMPLOYMENT

AFTER A unique 25-year period of great prosperity the economy of the Western world has arrived at a critical point. I expect that the experience of the period will enter history under the name of The Great Prosperity as the 1930s are known as The Great Depression. We have indeed succeeded, by eliminating all the automatic brakes which operated in the past, namely the gold standard and fixed rates of exchange, in maintaining the full and even over-employment which was created by an expansion of credit and in the end prolonged by open inflation, for a much longer time than I should have thought possible. But the inevitable end is now near, if it has not already arrived.

I find myself in an unpleasant situation. I had preached for forty years that the time to prevent the coming of a depression is the boom. During the boom nobody listened to me. Now people again turn to me and ask how the consequences of a policy of which I had constantly warned can be avoided. I must witness the heads of the governments of all the Western industrial countries promising their people that they will stop the inflation *and* preserve full employment. But I know that they *cannot* do this. I even fear that such attempts, as President Ford has just announced, to postpone the inevitable crisis by a new inflationary push, may temporarily succeed and make the eventual breakdown even worse.

Three choices in policy
The disquieting but unalterable truth is that a false monetary and

---

* A revised version of a lecture delivered on 8 February, 1975, to the 'Convegno Internazionale: Il Problema della Moneta Oggi', organised in commemoration of the 100th birthday of Luigi Einaudi by the Academia Nazionale dei Lincei at Rome, and to be published in the proceedings of that congress.

[15]

credit policy, pursued through almost the whole period since the last war, has placed the economic systems of all the Western industrial countries in a highly unstable position in which *anything* we can do will produce most unpleasant consequences. We have a choice between only three possibilities:

– to allow a rapidly accelerating open inflation to continue until it has brought about a complete disorganisation of all economic activity;

– to impose controls of wages and prices which will for a time conceal the effects of a continued inflation but would inevitably lead to a centrally-directed totalitarian economic system; and

– finally, to terminate resolutely the increase of the quantity of money which would soon, through the appearance of substantial unemployment, make manifest all the misdirections of labour which the inflation of the past years has caused and which the two other procedures would further increase.

Lessons of the Great Inflation

To understand why the whole Western world allowed itself to be led into this frightful dilemma, it is necessary to glance briefly back at two events soon after the First World War which have largely determined the views that have governed the policy of the post-war years. I want first to recall an experience which has unfortunately been largely forgotten. In Austria and Germany the Great Inflation had directed our attention to the connection between changes in the quantity of money and changes in the degree of employment. It especially showed us that the employment created by inflation diminished as soon as the inflation slowed down, and that the termination of the inflation always produced what came to be called a 'stabilisation crisis' with substantial unemployment. It was the insight into this connection which made me and some of my contemporaries from the outset reject and oppose the kind of full employment policy propagated by Lord Keynes and his followers.

I do not want to leave this recollection of the Great Inflation without adding that I have probably learnt at least as much if not more than I learnt from personally observing it by being taught to see – then largely by my teacher, the late Ludwig von Mises – the utter stupidity of the arguments then propounded, especially in Germany, to explain and justify the increases in the quantity of money. Most of these arguments I am now encountering again in countries, not least Britain and the USA, which then seemed economically better trained and whose economists rather looked down at the foolishness of the German economists. None of these apologists of the inflationary policy was able to propose or apply measures to terminate the inflation, which was finally ended by a man, Hjalmar Schacht, who firmly believed in a crude and primitive version of the quantity theory.

British origin of inflation as cure for unemployment
The policy of the recent decades, or the theory which underlies it, had its origin, however, in the specific experiences of Great Britain during the 1920s and 1930s. Great Britain had after what now seems the very modest inflation of the First World War, returned to the gold standard in 1925, in my opinion very sensibly and honestly, but unfortunately and unwisely at the former parity. This had in no way been required by classical doctrine: David Ricardo had in 1821 written to a friend[1] that 'I never should advise a government to restore a currency, which was depreciated 30 per cent, to par'. I ask myself often how different the economic history of the world might have been if, in the discussion of the years preceding 1925, even only one English economist had remembered and pointed out this long-published passage from Ricardo.

In the event, the unfortunate decision taken in 1925 made a prolonged process of deflation inevitable, which process might have been successful in maintaining the gold standard if it had been continued until a large part of the wages had been reduced. I believe this attempt was near success when in the world crisis of 1931 Britain abandoned it together with the gold standard, which was greatly discredited by this event.

---

[1] David Ricardo to John Wheatley, 18 September, 1821, reprinted in *The Works of David Ricardo*, ed. Piero Sraffa, Cambridge University Press, Vol. IX, 1952, p. 73.

II
KEYNES' POLITICAL 'CURE' FOR UNEMPLOYMENT
Development of Keynesian ideas

IT WAS during the period of extensive unemployment in Great Britain preceding the world-wide economic crisis of 1929–31 that John Maynard Keynes developed his basic ideas. It is important to note that this development of his economic thought happened in a very exceptional and almost unique position of his country. It was a period when, as a result of the big appreciation of the international value of the pound sterling, the real wages of practically all British workers had been substantially increased compared with the rest of the world, and British exporters had in consequence become substantially unable successfully to compete with other countries. In order to give employment to the unemployed it would therefore have been necessary either to reduce practically *all* wages or to raise the sterling prices of most commodities.

In the development of Keynes' thought it is possible to distinguish three distinct phases. First, he began with the recognition that it was necessary to reduce real wages. Second, he arrived at the conclusion that this was *politically* impossible. Third, he convinced himself that it would be vain and even harmful. The Keynes of 1919 had still understood that:

'There is no subtler, no surer means of overturning the existing basis of society than to debauch the currency. The process engages all the hidden forces of economic law on the side of destruction, and does it in a manner which not one man in a million is able to diagnose.'[1]

His political judgement made him the inflationist, or at least avid anti-deflationist, of the 1930s. I have, however, good reason to believe that he would have disapproved of what his followers did in the post-war period. If he had not died so soon, he would have become one of the leaders in the fight against inflation.

'The fatal idea'

It was in that unfortunate episode of English monetary history in

[1] *The Economic Consequences of the Peace* (1919), reprinted in *The Collected Writings of John Maynard Keynes*, Macmillan for the Royal Economic Society, Vol. II, 1971, p. 149.

which he became the intellectual leader that he gained acceptance for the fatal idea: that unemployment is predominantly due to an insufficiency of aggregate demand compared with the total of wages which would have to be paid if all workers were employed at current rates.

This formula of employment as a direct function of total demand proved so extraordinarily effective because it seemed to be confirmed in some degree by the results of quantitative empirical data. In contrast, the alternative explanations of unemployment which I regard as correct could make no such claims. The dangerous effects which the 'scientistic' prejudice has had in this diagnosis is the subject of my Nobel lecture at Stockholm (Part II). Briefly, we find the curious situation that the (Keynesian) theory, which is comparatively best confirmed by statistics because it happens to be the only one which can be tested quantitatively, is nevertheless false. Yet it is widely accepted only because the explanation earlier regarded as true, and which I still regard as true, cannot *by its very nature* be tested by statistics.

III
The True Theory of Unemployment

THE TRUE, though untestable, explanation of extensive unemployment ascribes it to a discrepancy between the distribution of labour (and the other factors of production) between industries (and localities) and the distribution of demand among their products. This discrepancy is caused by a distortion of the system of *relative* prices and wages. And it can be corrected only by a change in these relations, that is, by the establishment in each sector of the economy of those prices and wages at which supply will equal demand.

The cause of unemployment, in other words, is a deviation from the equilibrium prices and wages which would establish themselves with a free market and stable money. But we can never know beforehand at what structure of relative prices and wages such an equilibrium would establish itself. We are therefore unable to measure the deviation of current prices from the equilibrium prices which make it impossible to sell part of the labour supply. We are therefore also unable to demonstrate a statistical correlation between the distortion of relative prices and the volume of unemployment. Yet, although not measurable, causes may be very effective. The current superstition that only the measurable can be important has done much to mislead economists and the world in general.

Keynes' temptations to the politicians
Probably even more important than the fashionable prejudices concerning scientific method which made the Keynesian theory attractive to professional economists were the temptations it held out for politicians. It offered them not only a cheap and quick method of removing a chief source of real human suffering. It also promised them release from the most confining restrictions that had impeded them in their striving for popularity. Spending money and budget deficits were suddenly represented as virtues. It was even argued persuasively that increased government expenditure was wholly meritorious, since it led to the utilisation of hitherto unused resources and thus cost the community nothing but brought it a net gain.

These beliefs led in particular to the gradual removal of all effective barriers to an increase in the quantity of money by the monetary authorities. The Bretton Woods agreement had tried to place the burden of international adjustment exclusively on the surplus countries, that is, to require them to expand but not to require the deficit countries to contract. It thus laid the foundation for a world inflation. But this was at least done in the laudable endeavour to secure fixed rates of exchange. Yet when the criticism of the inflation-minded majority of economists succeeded in removing this last obstacle to national inflation, no effective brake remained, as the experience of Britain since the late 1960s illustrates.

Floating exchanges, full employment, stable currency
It is, I believe, undeniable that the demand for flexible rates of exchange originated wholly from countries such as Britain some of whose economists wanted a wider margin for inflationary expansion (called 'full employment policy'). They have, unfortunately, later received support also from other economists who were not inspired by the desire for inflation but who seem to me to have overlooked the strongest argument in favour of fixed rates of exchange: that they constitute the practically irreplaceable curb

[20]

we need to *compel* the politicians, and the monetary authorities responsible to them, to maintain a stable currency. The maintenance of the value of money and the avoidance of inflation constantly demand from the politicians highly unpopular measures which they can justify to people adversely affected only by showing that government was compelled to take them. So long as the preservation of the external value of the national currency is regarded as an indisputable necessity, as it is with fixed exchange rates, politicians can resist the constant demands for cheaper credits, avoidance of a rise in interest rates, more expenditure on 'public works', and so on. With fixed exchanges a fall in the foreign value of the currency or an outflow of gold or foreign exchange reserves acted as a signal requiring prompt government action. With flexible exchange rates, the effect of an increase in the quantity of money on the internal price level is much too slow to be generally recognised or to be charged to those ultimately responsible for it. Moreover, the inflation of prices is usually preceded by a welcome increase in employment, and it may therefore even be welcomed because its harmful effects are not visible until later.

It is therefore easy to understand why, in the hope of restraining countries all too inclined towards inflation, others like Germany, even while noticeably suffering from imported inflation, hesitated in the post-war period to destroy altogether the system of fixed rates of exchange. For a time it seemed likely to restrain the temptation further to speed up inflation. But now that the system of fixed rates of exchange appears to have totally collapsed, and there is scarcely any hope that self-discipline might induce some countries to restrain themselves, little reason is left to adhere to a system that is no longer effective. In retrospect one may even ask whether, out of a mistaken hope, the German Bundesbank or the Swiss National Bank have not waited too long, and then raised the value of their currency too little. But in the long run I do not believe we shall regain a system of international stability without returning to a system of fixed exchange rates which imposes upon the national central banks the restraint essential if they are successfully to resist the pressure of the inflation-minded forces of their countries – usually including Ministers of Finance.

IV
Inflation Ultimately Increases Unemployment

But why all this fear of inflation? Should we not try to learn to live with it, as some South American States seem to have done, particularly if, as some believe, this is necessary to secure full employment? If this were true and the harm done by inflation were only that which many people emphasise, we would have to consider this possibility seriously.

Why we cannot live with inflation

The answer, however, is twofold. *First,* such inflation, in order to achieve the goal aimed at, would have constantly to *accelerate,* and accelerating inflation would sooner or later reach a degree which makes all effective order of a market economy impossible. *Second,* and most important, in the long run such inflation makes much *more* unemployment inevitable than that which it was originally designed to prevent.

The argument often advanced that inflation produces merely a *redistribution* of the social product, while unemployment *reduces* it and therefore represents a worse evil, is thus false, because *inflation becomes the cause of increased unemployment.*

Harmful effects of inflation

I certainly do not wish to under-estimate the other harmful effects of inflation. They are much worse than anyone can conceive who has not himself lived through a great inflation. I count my first eight months in a job during which my salary rose to 200 times the initial amount as such an experience. I am indeed convinced that such a mismanagement of the currency is tolerated by the people only because, while the inflation proceeds, nobody has the time or energy to organise a popular rebellion.

What I want to say is that even the effects which every citizen experiences are not the worst consequence of inflation, which is usually not understood because *it becomes visible only when the inflation is past.* This must particularly be said to economists, politicians or others who like to point to the South American countries which have had inflations lasting through several generations and seem to have learnt to live with them. In these predominantly agrarian countries the effects of inflation are chiefly limited to those mentioned. The most serious effects that inflation produces in the labour markets of industrial countries are of minor importance in South America.

The attempts made in some of these countries, in particular Brazil, to deal with the problems of inflation by some method of indexing can, at best, remedy some of the consequences but certainly not the chief causes or the most harmful effects. They could not prevent the worst damage which inflation causes, that misdirection of labour which I must now consider more fully.

The misdirection of labour

Inflation makes certain jobs *temporarily* attractive. They will disappear when it stops or even when it ceases to accelerate at a sufficient rate. This result follows because inflation

(a) changes the distribution of the money stream between the various sectors and stages of the process of production, and

(b) creates expectation of a further rise of prices.

The defenders of a monetary full employment policy often represent the position as if a *single* increase of total demand were sufficient to secure full employment for an indefinite but fairly long period. This argument overlooks both the inevitable effects of such a policy on the distribution of labour between industries and those on the wage policy of the trade unions.

As soon as government assumes the responsibility to maintain full employment at whatever wages the trade unions succeed in obtaining, they no longer have any reason to take account of the unemployment their wage demands might have caused. In this situation every rise of wages which exceeds the increase in productivity will make necessary an increase in total demand if unemployment is not to ensue. The increase in the quantity of money made necessary by the upward movement of wages thus released becomes a *continuous* process requiring a constant influx of additional quantities of money. The additional money supply must lead to changes in the relative strength of demand for various kinds of goods and services. And these changes in relative demand must lead to further changes in relative prices and consequent changes in the direction of production and the allocation of the factors of production, including labour. I must leave

aside here all the other reasons why the prices of different goods
– and the quantities produced – will react differently to changes in
the demand (such as elasticities – the speed with which supply
can respond to demand).

The chief conclusion I want to demonstrate is that the longer
the inflation lasts, the larger will be the number of the workers
whose jobs depend on a *continuation* of the inflation, often even on
a continuing *acceleration* of the rate of inflation – not because
they would not have found employment without the inflation,
but because they were drawn by the inflation into *temporarily*
attractive jobs which after a slowing down or cessation of the
inflation will again disappear.

The consequences are unavoidable

We ought to have no illusion that we can escape the consequences
of the mistakes we have made.[1] Any attempt to preserve the
jobs made profitable by inflation would lead to a complete destruction of the market order. *We have once again in the post-war
period missed the opportunity to forestall a depression while there
was still time to do so.* We have indeed used our emancipation
from institutional restraints – the gold standard and fixed exchange
rates – to act more stupidly than ever before.

But if we cannot escape the re-appearance of substantial
unemployment, this is not the effect of a failure of 'capitalism' or
the market economy, but exclusively due to our own errors which
past experience and available knowledge ought to have enabled us
to avoid. It is unfortunately only too true that the disappointment
of expectations they have created may lead to serious social
unrest. But this does not mean that we can avoid it. The most
serious danger now is certainly that attempts, so attractive for the
politicians, to postpone the evil day and thereby make things in
the long run even worse, may still succeed. I must confess I
have been wishing for some time that the inescapable crisis may
come soon. And I hope now that any attempts made promptly to

---

[1] I should make it clear that, although I was addressing an audience in Italy,
what I am saying certainly also applies to Britain and most other Western
countries. There is little sign so far of this truth being understood in Britain. –
F.A.H.

restart the process of monetary expansion will not succeed, and that we shall now be forced to face the choice of a new policy.

Temporary, not mass, unemployment

Let me, however, emphasise at once that, although I regard a period of some months, perhaps even more than a year, of considerable unemployment as unavoidable, this does not mean that we must expect another long period of mass unemployment comparable with the Great Depression of the 1930s, provided we do not commit very bad mistakes of policy. Such a development can be prevented by a sensible policy which does not repeat the errors responsible for the duration of the Great Depression.

But before I turn to what our future policy ought to be I want to reject emphatically a misrepresentation of my point of view. I certainly do not recommend unemployment as a *means* to combat inflation. But I have to advise in a situation in which *the choice open to us is solely between some unemployment in the near future and more unemployment at a later date.* What I fear above all is the *apres nous la deluge* attitude of the politicians who in their concern about the next elections are likely to choose more unemployment later. Unfortunately even some commentators, such as the writers of the *Economist*, argue in a similar manner and have called for 'reflation' when the increase in the quantity of money is still continuing.

V

WHAT CAN BE DONE NOW?

The first step

THE FIRST necessity now is to stop the increase of the quantity of money – or at least to reduce it to the rate of the real growth of production – and this cannot happen soon enough. Moreover, *I can see no advantage in a gradual deceleration,* although for purely technical reasons it may prove all we can achieve.

It does not follow that we should not endeavour to stop a real deflation when it threatens to set in. Although I do not regard deflation as the original cause of a decline in business activity, a disappointment of expectations has unquestionably tended to induce a process of deflation – what more than 40 years ago I

[25]

called a 'secondary deflation'[1] – the effect of which may be worse, and in the 1930s certainly was worse, than what the original cause of the reaction made necessary, and which has no steering function to perform.

I have to confess that 40 years ago I argued differently. I have since altered my opinion – not about the theoretical explanation of the events but about the practical possibility of removing the obstacles to the functioning of the system by allowing deflation to proceed for a while.

I then believed that a short process of deflation might break the rigidity of money wages (what economists have since come to call their 'rigidity downwards') or the resistance to the reduction of some particular money wages, and that in this way we could restore relative wages determined by the market. This seems to me still an indispensable condition if the market mechanism is to function satisfactorily. But I no longer believe it is in practice possible to achieve it in this manner. I probably should have seen then that the last chance was lost after the British government in 1931 abandoned the attempt to bring costs down by deflation just when it seemed near success.

Prevent recession degenerating into depression
If I were today responsible for the monetary policy of a country I would certainly try to prevent a threatening deflation, that is, an absolute decrease of the stream of incomes, by all suitable means, and would announce that I intended to do so. This alone would probably be sufficient to prevent a degeneration of the recession into a long-lasting depression. The re-establishment of a properly functioning market would however still require a re-structuring of the whole system of relative prices and wages and a re-adjustment to the expectation of stable prices, which presupposes a much greater flexibility of wages than exists now. What chance we have to achieve such a determination of relative wage-rates by the market and how long it may take I dare not predict. But, although I recognise that a *general* reduction of money wages is politically unachievable, I am still convinced that the required adjustment of the structure of *relative* wages can be

[1] Defined and discussed in Part III, p. 44. I recall that the phrase was frequently used in the LSE Seminar from the 1930s.

achieved without inflation only through the reduction of the money wages of some groups of workers, and therefore must be thus achieved.

From a longer point of view it is obvious that, once we have got over the immediate difficulties, we must not avail ourselves again of the seemingly cheap and easy method of achieving full employment by aiming at the maximum of employment which in the short run can be achieved by monetary pressure.

The Keynesian dream

The Keynesian dream is gone even if its ghost will continue to plague politics for decades. It is to be wished, though this is clearly too much to hope for, that the term 'full employment' itself, which has become so closely associated with the inflationist policy, should be abandoned – or that we should at least remember that it was the aim of classical economists long before Keynes. John Stuart Mill reports in his autobiography[1] how 'full employment with high wages' appeared to him in his youth as the chief *desideratum* of economic policy.

The primary aim: stable money, not unstable 'full' employment

What we must now be clear about is that our aim must be, not the maximum of employment which can be achieved in the short run, but a 'high and stable [i.e. *continuing*] level of employment', as one of the wartime British White Papers on employment policy phrased it.[2] This however we can achieve only through the re-establishment of a properly functioning market which, by the free play of prices and wages, establishes for each sector the correspondence of supply and demand.

Though it must remain one of the chief tasks of monetary policy to prevent wide fluctuations in the quantity of money or the volume of the income stream, the effect on employment must not be the dominating consideration guiding it. *The primary aim must again become the stability of the value of money.* The currency authorities must again be effectively protected against the political

[1] *Autobiography and other Writings*, ed. J. Stillinger, Houghton Mifflin, Boston, 1969.

[2] *Employment Policy*, Cmd. 6527, HMSO, May 1944, Foreword.

pressure which today forces them so often to take measures that are politically advantageous in the short run but harmful to the community in the long run.

Disciplining the monetary authorities

I wish I could share the confidence of my friend Milton Friedman who thinks that one could deprive the monetary authorities, in order to prevent the abuse of their powers for political purposes, of all discretionary powers by prescribing the amount of money they may and should add to circulation in any one year. It seems to me that he regards this as practicable because he has become used for statistical purposes to draw a sharp distinction between what is to be regarded as money and what is not. This distinction does not exist in the real world. I believe that, to ensure the convertibility of all kinds of near-money into real money, which is necessary if we are to avoid severe liquidity crises or panics, the monetary authorities must be given some discretion. But I agree with Friedman that we will have to try and get back to a more or less automatic system for regulating the quantity of money in ordinary times. His principle is one that monetary authorities ought to aim at, not one to which they ought to be tied by law. The necessity of 'suspending' Sir Robert Peel's Bank Act of 1844 three times within 25 years after it was passed ought to have taught us this once and for all.

And although I am not as optimistic as the Editor of the London *Times*, Mr William Rees-Mogg, who in a sensational article[1] (and now in a book)[2] has proposed the return to the gold standard, it does make me feel somewhat more optimistic when I see such a proposal coming from so influential a source. I would even agree that among the feasible monetary systems the international gold standard is the best, if I could believe that the most important countries could be trusted to obey the rules of the game necessary for its preservation. But this seems to me exceedingly unlikely, and no single country can have an effective gold standard: by its

---

[1] 'Crisis of Paper Currencies: Has the Time Come for Britain to Return to the Gold Standard?', *The Times*, 1 May, 1974.

[2] *The Reigning Error. The Crisis of World Inflation*, Hamish Hamilton, London, 1974.

nature it is an international system and can function only as an international system.

It is, however, a big step in the direction of a return to reason when at the end of his book Mr Rees-Mogg argues that

'We should be tearing up the full employment commitment of the 1944 White Paper, a great political and economic revolution.

'This would until very recently have seemed a high price to pay; now it is no great price at all. There is little or no prospect of maintaining full employment with the present inflation, in Britain or in the world. The full employment standard became a commitment to inflation, but the inflation has now accelerated past the point at which it is compatible with full employment.'[1]

Equally encouraging is a statement of the British Chancellor of the Exchequer, Mr Denis Healey, who is reported to have said:

'It is far better that more people should be in work, *even if that means accepting lower wages on average,* than that those lucky enough to keep their jobs should scoop the pool while millions are living on the dole'.[2] (My italics.)

It would almost seem as if in Britain, the country in which the harmful doctrines originated, a reversal of opinion were now under way. Let us hope it will rapidly spread over the world.

[1] *Ibid.*, p. 112.

[2] Speech at East Leeds Labour Club reported in *The Times*, 11 January, 1975.

PART II

The Pretence of Knowledge *

THE PARTICULAR occasion of this lecture, combined with the chief practical problem which economists have to face today, have made the choice of its topic almost inevitable. On the one hand, the still recent establishment of the Nobel Memorial Prize in Economic Sciences marks a significant step in the process by which, in the opinion of the general public, economics has been conceded some of the dignity and prestige of the physical sciences. On the other hand, economists are at this moment called upon to say how to extricate the free world from the serious threat of accelerating inflation which, it must be admitted, has been brought about by policies the majority of economists have recommended and even urged governments to pursue. We have indeed at the moment little cause for pride: as a profession we have made a mess of things.

The 'scientistic' attitude derived from the physical sciences[1]
It seems to me that this failure of economists to guide policy more successfully is closely connected with their propensity to imitate as closely as possible the procedures of the brilliantly successful physical sciences – an attempt which in our subject may lead to outright error. It is an approach that has come to be described as the 'scientistic' attitude – which, as I defined it some 30 years ago,

> 'is decidedly unscientific in the true sense of the word, since it involves a mechanical and uncritical application of habits of thought to fields different from those in which they have been formed.'[2]

---

* Alfred Nobel Memorial Lecture delivered on 11 December, 1974, at the Stockholm School of Economics. © Copyright the Nobel Foundation, Stockholm.

[1] [The sub-headings have been inserted to help readers, especially non-economists unfamiliar with Professor Hayek's writings, to follow the argument; they were not part of the original Nobel Lecture. – ED.]

[2] 'Scientism and the Study of Society', *Economica*, August 1942, reprinted in *The Counter-Revolution of Science*, Glencoe, Ill., 1952, p. 15 of this reprint.

I want to begin by explaining how some of the gravest errors of recent economic policy are a direct consequence of this scientistic error.

The theory which has been guiding monetary and financial policy during the last 30 years, and which I contend is largely the product of such a mistaken conception of the proper scientific procedure, consists in the assertion that there exists a simple positive correlation between total employment and the size of the aggregate demand for goods and services; and it leads to the belief that we can permanently ensure full employment by maintaining total money expenditure at an appropriate level. Among the various theories advanced to account for extensive unemployment, this is probably the only one in support of which strong quantitative evidence can be adduced. I nevertheless regard it as fundamentally false, and to act upon it, as we now experience, as very harmful.

This brings me to the crucial issue. Unlike the position in the physical sciences, in economics and other disciplines that deal with what I call 'essentially complex' phenomena, the aspects of the events to be explained for which we can obtain quantitative data are necessarily limited and may not include the important ones. While in the physical sciences it is generally assumed, probably with good reason, that any important factor which determines the observed events will itself be directly observable and measurable, in the study of such 'essentially complex' phenomena as the market, which depend on the actions of many individuals, all the circumstances that will determine the outcome of a process, for reasons I shall explain later, *will hardly ever be fully known or measurable*. And while in the physical sciences the investigator will be able to measure, on the basis of a *prima facie* theory, what he thinks important, in the social sciences what is treated as important is often that which happens to be accessible to measurement. This is sometimes carried to the point where it is demanded that our theories must be formulated in such terms that they refer only to measurable magnitudes.

It can hardly be denied that such a demand quite arbitrarily limits the facts that are to be admitted as possible causes of the events in the real world. This view, which is often quite naively accepted as required by scientific procedure, has some rather paradoxical consequences. We know, of course, about the market and similar social structures, very many facts that we cannot measure and on which indeed we have only some very imprecise and general information. And because the effects of these facts in any particular instance cannot be confirmed by quantitative evidence, they are simply disregarded by those sworn to admit only what they regard as scientific evidence. And they thereupon happily proceed on the fiction that the factors they can measure are the only relevant ones.

The correlation between aggregate demand and total employment, for instance, may be only approximate; but as it is the *only* one on which we have quantitative data, it is accepted as the only causal connection that counts. On this standard there may thus well exist better 'scientific' evidence for a false theory, which will be accepted because it appears as more 'scientific', than for a valid explanation, which is rejected because there is no sufficient quantitative evidence for it.

The chief cause of unemployment
Let me illustrate this by a brief sketch of what I regard as the chief true cause of extensive unemployment – an account which will also explain why such unemployment cannot be lastingly cured by the inflationary policies recommended by the now fashionable theory. The correct explanation appears to me to be the existence of discrepancies between the distribution of demand among the different goods and services and the allocation of labour and other resources among the production of those outputs. We possess a fairly good 'qualitative' knowledge of the forces by which a correspondence between demand and supply in the different sectors of the economic system is brought about, of the conditions under which it will be achieved, and of the factors likely to prevent such an adjustment. The separate steps in the account of this process rely on facts of everyday experience, and few who take the trouble to follow the argument will question the validity of the factual assumptions, or the logical correctness of the conclusions drawn from them. We have indeed good reason to believe that unemployment indicates that the structure of *relative* prices and wages has been distorted (usually by monopolistic or governmental price-fixing), and that to restore equality between the demand for and the supply of labour in all sectors changes of

relative prices and wages and some transfers of labour will be necessary.

But when we are asked for quantitative evidence for the particular structure of prices and wages that would be required to assure a smooth continuous sale of the products and services offered, we must admit that we have no such information. We know, in other words, the *general* conditions in which what we call, somewhat misleadingly, an 'equilibrium' will establish itself: but we never know the *particular* prices or wages that would exist if the market were to bring about such an equilibrium. We can merely say in which conditions we can expect the market to establish prices and wages at which demand will equal supply. But we can never produce statistical information that would show how much the prevailing prices and wages *deviate* from those that would secure a continuous sale of the current supply of labour. This account of the causes of unemployment is an empirical theory, in the sense that it might be proved false: for example, if with a constant money supply, a general increase of wages did not lead to unemployment. But it is certainly not the kind of theory we could use to obtain specific numerical predictions concerning the rates of wages, or the distribution of labour, to be expected.

Why should we in economics, however, have to plead ignorance of the sort of facts on which, in the case of a physical theory, a scientist would certainly be expected to give precise information? It is probably not surprising that people impressed by the example of the physical sciences should find this position very unsatisfactory and should insist on the standards of proof they find there. The reason for this state of affairs, as I have briefly indicated, is that the social sciences, like much of biology but unlike most of the physical sciences, have to deal with structures of *essential* complexity, that is, whose characteristic properties can be exhibited only by models made up of relatively large numbers of variables. Competition, for example, is a process which will produce certain results only if it proceeds among a fairly *large* number of acting persons.

In some inquiries, particularly where problems of a similar kind arise in the physical sciences, the difficulties can be overcome by using, not specific information about the individual elements, but data about the relative frequency, or the probability, of the occurrence of the various distinctive properties of the elements. But this is true only where we have to deal with what has been called by Dr Warren Weaver (formerly of the Rockefeller Foundation), with a distinction that ought to be much more widely understood, 'phenomena of unorganised complexity', in contrast to those 'phenomena of organised complexity' with which we have to deal in the social sciences.[1] Organised complexity here means that the character of the structures showing it depends not only on the properties of the individual elements of which they are composed, and the relative frequency with which they occur, but also on the manner in which the individual elements are connected with one another. In explaining the working of such structures we cannot for this reason replace the information about the individual elements by statistical information, but require full information about each element if from our theory we are to derive specific predictions about individual events. Without such specific information about the individual elements we shall be confined to what on another occasion I have called mere 'pattern predictions' – predictions of some of the general attributes of the structures that will form themselves, but not containing specific statements about the individual elements of which the structures will be made up.[2]

This is particularly true of our theories accounting for the determination of the systems of relative prices and wages that will form themselves on a well-functioning market. Into the determination of these prices and wages will enter the effects of particular information possessed by every one of the participants in the market process – a sum of facts which in their totality cannot be known to the scientific observer or to any other single brain. It is indeed the source of the superiority of the market order, and the reason why, so long as it is not suppressed by the powers of government, it regularly displaces other types of

[1] Warren Weaver, 'A Quarter Century in the Natural Sciences', *The Rockefeller Foundation Annual Report 1958*, Ch. I, 'Science and Complexity'.

[2] Cf. my essay, 'The Theory of Complex Phenomena', in M. Bunge (ed.), *The Critical Approach to Science and Philosophy. Essays in Honor of K. R. Popper*, New York, 1964, and reprinted (with additions) in my *Studies in Philosophy, Politics and Economics*, Routledge & Kegan Paul, London and University of Chicago Press, Chicago, 1967.

order, that in the resulting allocation of resources it uses more of the knowledge of particular facts which exists only dispersed among uncounted persons, than any one person can possess. But because we, the observing scientists, can thus never *know* all the determinants of such an order, and in consequence also cannot know at which particular structure of prices and wages demand would everywhere equal supply, we also cannot measure the deviations from that order. Nor can we statistically test our theory that it is the deviations from that 'equilibrium' system of prices and wages which makes it impossible to sell certain products and services at the prices at which they are offered.

Mathematical method in economics: uses and limitations
Before I continue with my immediate concern, the effects of all this on the employment policies currently pursued, allow me to define more specifically the inherent limitations of our numerical knowledge that are so often overlooked. I want to do this to avoid giving the impression that I generally reject the mathematical method in economics. I regard it indeed as the great advantage of the mathematical technique that it allows us to describe, by algebraic equations, the general character of a pattern even where we are ignorant of the numerical values determining its particular manifestation. Without this algebraic technique we could scarcely have achieved that comprehensive picture of the *mutual inter-dependencies* of the different events in a market. It has, however, led to the illusion that we can use this technique to determine and predict the *numerical values* of those magnitudes; and this has led to a vain search for quantitative or numerical constants.

This happened despite that the modern founders of mathematical economics had no such illusions. It is true their systems of equations describing the pattern of a market equilibrium are so framed that, *if* we were able to fill in all the blanks of the abstract formulae, that is, *if* we knew all the parameters of these equations, we could calculate the prices and quantities of all commodities and services sold. But, as Vilfredo Pareto, one of the founders of this theory, clearly stated, its purpose cannot be 'to arrive at a numerical calculation of prices' because, as he said, it would be 'absurd' to assume that we could ascertain all the data.[1] Indeed, the chief

[1] V. Pareto, *Manuel d'economie politique*, 2nd edn., Paris, 1927, pp. 223–4.

[35]

point was seen by those remarkable anticipators of modern economics, the Spanish schoolmen of the 16th century, who emphasised that what they called *pretium mathematicum*, the mathematical price, depended on so many particular circumstances that it could never be known to man but was known only to God.[1] I sometimes wish that our mathematical economists would take this to heart. I must confess that I still doubt whether their search for measurable magnitudes has made significant contributions to our *theoretical understanding* of economic phenomena – as distinct from their value as a *description* of particular situations. Nor am I prepared to accept the excuse that this branch of research is still very young: Sir William Petty, the founder of econometrics, was after all a somewhat senior colleague of Sir Isaac Newton in the Royal Society![2]

There may be few instances in which the superstition that only measurable magnitudes can be important has done positive harm in the economic field; but the present problem of inflation and employment is a very serious one. Its effect has been that what is generally the true cause of extensive unemployment has been disregarded by the scientistically-minded majority of economists, because its operation could not be confirmed by directly observable relations between measurable magnitudes. Instead, an almost exclusive concentration on quantitatively measurable *surface* phenomena has produced a policy that has made matters worse.

It has, of course, to be readily admitted that the kind of theory I regard as the true explanation of unemployment is of somewhat limited content because it allows us to make only very general predictions of the *kind* of events we must expect in a given situation. But the effects on policy of the more ambitious constructions have not been very fortunate. I confess that I prefer true but imperfect knowledge, even if it leaves much undetermined and unpredictable, to a pretence of exact knowledge that is likely to be false. The credit gained for seemingly simple but false theories by their apparent conformity with recognised scientific standards may, as the present instance shows, have grave consequences.

---

[1] Cf., e.g., Luis Molina, *De iustitia et iure*, Cologne, 1596–1600, tom. II, disp. 347, no. 3, and particularly Johannes de Lugo, *Disputationum de iustitia et iure tomus secundus*, Lyon, 1642, disp. 26, sect. 4, no. 40.

[2] [Petty: 1623–87; Newton: 1642–1727.-ED.]

Macro-economic solution for unemployment may cause resource-misallocation and intensify unemployment
Indeed, in the case discussed, the very measures which the dominant 'macro-economic' theory has recommended as a remedy for unemployment, namely the increase of aggregate demand, have become a cause of a very extensive misallocation of resources which is likely to make later large-scale unemployment inevitable. The continuous injection of additional amounts of money at points of the economic system where it creates a temporary demand which must cease when the increase of the quantity of money stops or slows down, together with the expectation of a continuing rise of prices, draws labour and other resources into employments which can last only so long as the increase of the quantity of money continues at the same rate – or perhaps even only so long as it continues to accelerate at a given rate. What this policy has produced is not so much a level of employment that could not have been brought about in other ways as a distribution of employment which cannot be maintained indefinitely and which after some time can be maintained only by a rate of inflation that would rapidly lead to a disorganisation of all economic activity. The truth is that by a mistaken theoretical view we have been led into a precarious position in which we cannot prevent substantial unemployment from re-appearing: not because, as my view is sometimes misrepresented, this unemployment is deliberately brought about as a means to combat inflation, but because it is now bound to occur as a deeply regrettable but *inescapable* consequence of the mistaken policies of the past as soon as inflation ceases to accelerate.

I must, however, now leave these problems of immediate practical importance introduced chiefly to illustrate the momentous consequences that may follow from errors concerning abstract problems of the philosophy of science. There is as much reason to be apprehensive about the long-run dangers created in a much wider field, by the uncritical acceptance of assertions which have the *appearance* of being scientific, as there is in the problems I have just discussed.

When science is unscientific
What I mainly wanted to show by the topical illustration is that,

certainly in my subject, but I believe also generally in the sciences of man, what looks superficially like the most scientific procedure is often the most unscientific, and, beyond this, that in these other activities there are definite limits to what we can expect science to achieve. This means that to entrust to science – or to deliberate control according to scientific principles – more than scientific method can achieve may have deplorable effects. The progress of the natural sciences in modern times has of course so much exceeded all expectations that any suggestion that there may be some limits to it is bound to arouse suspicion. This insight will be especially resisted by all who have hoped that our increasing power of prediction and control, generally regarded as the characteristic result of scientific advance, applied to the processes of society, would soon enable us to mould it entirely to our liking. It is indeed true that, in contrast to the exhilaration which the discoveries of the physical sciences tend to produce, the insights we gain from the study of society more often have a dampening effect on our aspirations; and it is perhaps not surprising that the more impetuous younger members of our profession are not always prepared to accept this truth. Yet the confidence in the unlimited power of science is only too often based on a false belief that the scientific method consists in the application of a ready-made technique, or in imitating the form rather than the substance of scientific procedure, as if one needed only to follow some cooking recipes to solve all social problems. It sometimes almost seems as if the *techniques* of science were more easily learnt than the *thinking* that shows us what the problems are and how to approach them.

The conflict between what, in its present mood, the public expects science to achieve in satisfaction of popular hopes and what is really in its power is a serious matter. Even if all true scientists recognised the limitations of what they can do in human affairs, so long as the public expects more there will always be some who will pretend, and perhaps honestly believe, that they can do more to meet popular demands than is really in their power. It is often difficult enough for the expert, and certainly in many instances impossible for the layman, to distinguish between justified and unjustified claims advanced in the name of science. The enormous publicity recently given by the media to a report

[38]

pronouncing in the name of science on *The Limits to Growth,* and the silence of the same media about the devastating criticism this report has received from the competent experts,[1] must make one feel somewhat apprehensive about the use to which the prestige of science can be put. But it is by no means only in economics that far-reaching claims are made for a more scientific direction of all human activities and the desirability of replacing spontaneous processes by 'conscious human control'. If I am not mistaken, psychology, psychiatry and some branches of sociology, and still more the so-called philosophy of history, are even more affected by what I have called the scientistic prejudice, and by specious claims of what science can achieve.[2]

If we are to safeguard the reputation of science, and to prevent the arrogation of knowledge based on a superficial similarity of procedure with that of the physical sciences, much effort will have to be directed toward debunking such arrogations, some of which have by now become the vested interests of established university departments. We cannot be grateful enough to such modern philosophers of science as Sir Karl Popper for giving us a test by which we can distinguish between what we may and may not accept as scientific – a test which I am sure some doctrines now widely accepted as scientific would not pass. There are some special problems, however, in connection with those essentially complex phenomena of which social structures are so important an instance, which make me wish to conclude by restating in more general terms the reasons why in these fields not only are there absolute obstacles to the prediction of specific events, but why to act as if we possessed scientific knowledge enabling us to transcend

---

[1] *The Limits to Growth: A Report of the Club of Rome's Project on the Predicament of Mankind,* New York, 1972; for a systematic examination of this document by a distinguished economist cf. Wilfred Beckerman, *In Defence of Economic Growth,* London, 1974, and, for a list of earlier criticisms by experts, Gottfried Haberler, *Economic Growth and Stability,* Los Angeles, 1974, who rightly calls their effect 'devastating'.

[2] I have given some illustrations of these tendencies in other subjects in my inaugural lecture as Visiting Professor at the University of Salzburg, *Die Irrtümer des Konstruktivismus und die Grundlagen legitimer Kritik gesellschaftlicher Gebilde,* Munich, 1970, now re-issued for the Walter Eucken Institute, at Freiburg im Breisgau, by J. C. B. Mohr, Tübingen, 1975.

them may itself become a serious obstacle to the advance of the human intellect.

The obstacles to prediction

The chief point we must remember is that the vast and rapid advance of the physical sciences took place in fields where it proved that explanation and prediction could be based on laws which accounted for the observed phenomena as functions of comparatively *few* variables – either particular facts or relative frequencies of events. This may even be the ultimate reason why we single out these realms as 'physical' in contrast to those more highly organised structures I have here called 'essentially complex' phenomena. There is no reason why the position must be the same in the latter as in the former fields. The difficulties we encounter in essentially complex phenomena are not, as one might at first suspect, difficulties about formulating theories to explain the observed events – although they also cause special difficulties about testing proposed explanations and therefore about eliminating bad theories. They are due to the chief problem which arises when we apply our theories to any particular situation in the real world. A theory of essentially complex phenomena must refer to a *large* number of particular facts, all of which must be ascertained before we can derive a prediction from it, or test it.

Once we succeeded in this task there should be no particular difficulty about deriving testable predictions. With the help of modern computers, it should be easy enough to insert these data into the appropriate blanks of the theoretical formulae and to derive a prediction. The real difficulty, to the solution of which science has *little* to contribute and which is sometimes indeed *insoluble*, consists in the ascertainment of the particular facts.

A simple example will show the nature of this difficulty. Consider a ball game played by a few people of approximately equal skill. If we knew a few particular facts in addition to our general knowledge of the ability of the individual players, such as their state of attention, their perceptions and the state of their hearts, lungs, muscles, etc. at each moment of the game, we could probably predict the outcome. Indeed, if we were familiar both with the game and the teams, we should probably have a fairly shrewd idea on what the outcome will depend. But we shall not of course be able to ascertain those facts, and in consequence the result of the game will be outside the range of the scientifically predictable however well we may know what effects particular events would have on the result of the game. This does not mean that we can make no predictions at all about the course of the game. If we know the rules of the different games we shall, in watching one, very soon know which game is being played, and what kinds of actions we can and cannot expect. But our capacity to predict will be confined to such *general* characteristics of the events to be expected, and will not include the capacity of predicting *particular* individual events.

This explanation corresponds to what I have called earlier the mere pattern predictions to which we are increasingly confined as we penetrate from the realm where relatively simple laws prevail into the range of phenomena where organised complexity rules. As we advance, we find more and more frequently that we can in practice ascertain some, but not all, of the particular circumstances which determine the outcome of a given process. In consequence, we are able to predict some, but not all, of the properties of the result we have to expect. Often all we shall be able to predict will be some abstract characteristic of the pattern that will appear – relations between kinds of elements about which individually we know very little. Yet, as I am anxious to repeat, we will still achieve predictions which can be falsified and which therefore satisfy Popper's test of empirical significance.

Of course, compared with the precise predictions we have learnt to expect in the physical sciences, this sort of mere pattern predictions is a second best with which we do not like to have to be content. Yet the danger against which I want to warn is precisely the belief that it is necessary to achieve more in order to have a claim to be accepted as scientific. This way lies charlatanism and worse. To act on the belief that we possess the knowledge and the power that enable us to shape the processes of society entirely to our liking, knowledge which in the real world we do *not* possess, is likely to make us do much harm.

Power to coerce may impede spontaneous forces
In the physical sciences there may be little objection to trying to do the impossible; we might even feel that we ought not to

discourage the over-confident because their experiments may after all produce new insights. But in the social sciences the erroneous belief that the exercise of some power would have beneficial consequences is likely to lead to a new power to *coerce* other men being conferred on some authority. Even if such power is not in itself bad, its exercise is likely to impede the functioning of those spontaneous ordering forces by which, without understanding them, man is in the real world so largely assisted in the pursuit of his aims. We are only beginning to understand on how subtle a communications system the functioning of an advanced industrial society is based. This communications system, which we call the market, turns out to be a more efficient mechanism for digesting dispersed information than any that man has deliberately designed.

If man is not to do more harm than good in his efforts to improve the social order, he will have to learn that, in this, as in all other fields where essential complexity of an organised kind prevails, *he cannot acquire the full knowledge which would make mastery of the events possible.* He will therefore have to use what knowledge he can achieve, not to shape the results as the craftsman shapes his handiwork, but rather to cultivate a growth by providing the appropriate environment, as the gardener does for his plants.

There is danger in the exuberant feeling of ever-growing power which the advance of the physical sciences has engendered and which tempts man to try – 'dizzy with success', to use a characteristic phrase of early communism – to subject not only our natural but also our human environment to the control of a human will. The recognition of the insuperable limits to his knowledge ought indeed to teach the student of society a lesson of humility which should guard him against becoming an accomplice in man's fatal striving to control society – a striving which makes him not only a tyrant over his fellows, but may well make him destroy a civilisation which no brain has designed but which has grown from the free efforts of millions of individuals.

PART III

No Escape: Unemployment Must Follow Inflation*

THE PRIMARY duty today of any economist who deserves the name seems to me to repeat on every occasion that the present unemployment is the direct and inevitable consequence of the so-called full employment policies pursued for the last 25 years. Most people still believe mistakenly that an increase in aggregate demand will remove unemployment for some time. Nothing therefore short of the realisation that this remedy, though usually effective in the short run, produces much more unemployment later will prevent the public from exerting irresistible pressure to resume inflation as soon as unemployment substantially increases.

To understand this basic truth is to recognise that the majority of economists whose advice governments have been following everywhere in Britain and the rest of the Western world during this period have thoroughly discredited themselves and ought to do penance in sackcloth and ashes. What was almost unquestioned orthodoxy for close to 30 years has been thoroughly discredited. And the present economic crisis also marks a severe setback in the authority of economics – or at least the long overdue collapse of the Keynesian bubble of the fashionable doctrine that has dominated opinion for a generation. I am fully convinced that before we can hope to return to reasonable stability, not to mention lasting prosperity, we must exorcise the Keynesian incubus. By this I mean less what John Maynard Keynes himself taught – because you can find in Keynes, as in Marx, almost anything – than the teaching of those Keynesians who, as Professor Joan Robinson recently wrote, 'sometimes had some trouble in getting Maynard to see what the point of his revolution really was'.[1]

* The following contains essentially additional points which I found necessary to insert in various lectures I gave during the month of April 1975 at various places in the United States on the general subject treated in Part I.

[1] Joan Robinson, 'What has become of the Keynesian Revolution?', in Milo Keynes (ed.), *Essays on John Maynard Keynes*, Cambridge University Press, 1975, p. 125.

Keynes confirmed business belief in high demand

The conquest of opinion by Keynesian economics is mainly due to the fact that its argument conformed with the age-old belief of the business man that his prosperity depended on consumers' demand. The plausible but erroneous conclusion derived from his individual experience in business that general prosperity could be maintained by keeping general demand high, against which economic theory had been arguing for generations, was suddenly again made respectable by Keynes. And since the 1930s it has been embraced as obvious good sense by a whole generation of economists brought up on the teaching of his school. It has had the effect that for a quarter of a century we have systematically employed all available methods of increasing money expenditure, which in the short run creates additional employment but at the same time leads to misdirections of labour that must ultimately result in extensive unemployment.

'Secondary depression' and monetary counter-measures

This fundamental connection between inflation and unemployment is obscured because, although (except during an actual deflation, i.e. a decrease of the quantity of money) insufficient demand is normally *not* the primary cause of unemployment, unemployment may itself become the cause of an absolute shrinkage of aggregate demand which in turn may bring about a further increase of unemployment and thus lead to a cumulative process of contraction in which unemployment feeds on unemployment. Such a 'secondary depression' caused by an induced deflation should of course be prevented by appropriate monetary counter-measures. (The difficult question, which I can only briefly mention here, is how this can be done without producing further misdirections of labour.) At this moment, however, our chief task is still to prevent attempts to combat the unemployment made inevitable through misdirections of labour by a renewed spurt of inflation, which would only increase these misdirections and thus in the long run make matters worse.

Difficult to discover the misdirected labour in 'the long prosperity'

A short exposition cannot do justice to the complexity of the facts in a further important problem. In past booms followed by depres-

[44]

sions the misdirections of labour were comparatively easy to trace because the expansion of credit during the boom served almost exclusively industrial investment. But during the recent long prosperity since the end of the war, which was maintained by the removal of all automatic checks on continued inflation (such as the gold standard, fixed exchange rates, relieving deficit countries from the necessity to contract, and providing extra international liquidity), the additional demand financed by inflation has been much more widely dispersed and is therefore much more difficult to trace. Its effect on the allocation of resources in general and especially of labour would have to be investigated separately for each country and part of the period; and I am by no means clear where the most important over-developments would be found. The places where the misplaced and in consequence now *dis*placed workers can find lasting employment can be discovered only by letting the market operate freely.

Revival must come from sustainable (profitable) investment

In general it is probably true to say that an equilibrium position will most effectively be approached if consumers' demand is prevented from falling substantially by providing employment through public works, from which workers will wish to move as soon as they can to other and better-paid occupations, not by directly stimulating investment and similar expenditure which will draw labour into jobs they will expect to be permanent but must cease as soon as the source of this expenditure dries up.

We must certainly expect the recovery to come from a revival of investment. But we want investment of the kind which will prove profitable and can be continued when a new position of fair stability and a high level of employment has been achieved. Neither a subsidisation of investment nor artificially low interest rates are likely to achieve this position. And least of all is the desirable (i.e. stable) form of investment to be brought about by stimulating consumers' demand.

The belief that, in order to make new investment profitable consumers' demand must increase is part of the same widespread fallacy to which the businessman is especially prone. It is true only of investment designed to increase output by using the *same* techniques as hitherto employed, but not of the only sort of investment which can increase productivity per head of worker by equipping a given labour force with *more* capital equipment. Such intensification of capital use is indeed encouraged by relatively *low* product (consumer good) prices (which make it necessary to save on labour costs) and discouraged by high ones. This is one of the elementary connections between wages and investment wholly overlooked in Keynesian economics.[1]

Monetarism and the mechanical (macro) quantity theory
The contention that a general rise of prices such as we in the Western world have experienced in recent years is wholly due to, and made possible solely by, an excessive increase in the quantity of money, and that, therefore, governmental monetary policy is wholly responsible for it, is today usually described as the 'monetarist' position. It seems to me in this general form incontrovertible, even though it is also true that what has led governments to such a policy was chiefly the activity of trade unions and similar activities by other monopolistic bodies (such as the oil cartel). But in a narrower sense 'monetarist' is today frequently used to describe the expositors of a somewhat mechanical form of the quantity theory of the value of money which in my opinion tends to over-simplify the theoretical argument.

My chief objection against this theory is that, as what is called a 'macro-theory', it pays attention only to the effect of changes in the quantity of money on the general price level and not to the effects on the structure of relative prices. In consequence, it tends to disregard what seem to me the most harmful effects of inflation, the misdirection of resources it causes and the unemployment which ultimately results from it.

Nevertheless, for most practical purposes I regard this simple form of the quantity theory as a decidedly helpful guide and agree that we should not forget that the great inflations of the past, particularly those in Germany of the early 1920s and the late 1940s, were effectively stopped by men[2] who acted on this somewhat crude form of the quantity theory. But, though this over-simplified explanation of events seems to me inadequate to

[1] [It is a central element in the Austrian theory of capital: Note, pp. 51–52. – ED.]

[2] Schacht and Erhard respectively.

account for some of the deleterious effects of changes in the quantity of money, I emphasised as long as nearly 45 years ago, when I attempted to remedy these defects, that

> 'it would be one of the worst things which could befall us if the general public should ever again cease to believe in the elementary propositions of the quantity theory'[1]

(then represented chiefly by the economists Irving Fisher and Gustav Cassel). But exactly this has happened as the result of the persuasive powers of Lord Keynes to whose proposals for combatting the depression of the 1930s the traditional views had been an obstacle.

Cantillon and Keynes

The defects of what became the traditional approach had indeed been pointed out 200 years earlier when Richard Cantillon had argued against John Locke's similar mechanical quantity theory that

> 'he realised well that the abundance of money makes everything dear, but he did not analyse how that takes place. The great difficulty of that analysis consists in the discovery by what path and in what proportion the increase of money raises the price of things.'[2]

This analysis Cantillon was the first to attempt, and in time the examination of the course through which an inflow of additional money alters the *relative* demand for different commodities and services led to an explanation of how inflation results in a misdirection of resources, and particularly labour which becomes 'redundant' as soon as inflation slows down or even ceases to accelerate. But this promising stream of thought was smothered by the Keynesian flood which threw economists back to a state of knowledge that had been surpassed long before, and re-opened the gates to errors of government policy of which our grandparents would have been ashamed.

---

[1] *Prices and Production*, London, Routledge, 1931, p. 3. E. von Böhm-Bawerk used to speak of 'the indestructible core of truth in the quantity theory'.

[2] Richard Cantillon, *An Essay on the Nature of Commerce in General*, ed. Henry Higgs, London, Macmillan, 1931, Part I, Chapter 6.

Present inflation engineered by government badly advised
The present inflation has been deliberately brought about by government on the advice of economists. The British Labour Party, as early as 1957, in its proposals for a National Pension Fund, dealt with the problem of future price movements by the assumption that prices would double between 1960 and 1980[1] – then an alarming prospect but now of course already far surpassed. As long ago as 1948 a highly influential textbook of economics[2] could plead that a 5 per cent per annum increase of prices was innocuous (which means that prices would double in less than 13 years). What these and other economists overlooked was that the purpose which they approved required an accelerating inflation, and that any accelerating inflation sooner or later becomes unbearable. Inflation at a constant rate soon comes to be anticipated in ordinary business transactions, and then merely harms the recipients of fixed contractual incomes but does no good.

'Inflation': true and false
Much confusion is of course caused in current discussion by a constant misuse of the term 'inflation'. Its original and proper meaning is an excessive increase of the quantity of money which will normally lead to an increase of prices. But even a general rise of prices, for instance one brought about by a shortage of food caused by bad harvests, is not inflation. Nor would a general rise of prices caused by a shortage of oil and other sources of energy that led to an absolute reduction of consumption be properly called inflation – if this shortage had not been made the excuse of a further increase in the quantity of money. There may also be considerable inflation that considerably harms the working of the market without any rise of prices – if this effect is prevented by controls. Indeed such a 'repressed' inflation tends to disorganise all economic activity even more than open inflation. Moreover it has no beneficial effects whatever even in the short run (except for

[1] *National Superannuation. Labour's Policy for Security in Old Age.* Published by the Labour Party, London, 1957, pp. 104 and 109.
[2] 'If price increases could be held down to, say, less than 5 per cent per year, such a mild steady inflation need not cause too great concern.' (Paul A. Samuelson, *Economics: An Introductory Analysis*, McGraw-Hill, First Edn., 1948, p. 282.)

the receivers of the additional money), and leads straight to a centrally directed economy.

Inflation and unemployment: over-eating and indigestion
Let me repeat in conclusion that inflation has of course many other bad effects, much more grave and painful than most people understand who have not lived through one; but that the most serious and at the same time the least understood is that in the long run it inevitably produces extensive unemployment. It is simply not true, as some economists have suggested, that so long as unemployment exists, an increase in aggregate demand does only good and no harm. That may be true in the short run but not in the long run. We do not have the choice between inflation and unemployment, as little as we can choose between over-eating and indigestion: though over-eating may be very pleasant while it proceeds, the indigestion will follow.

Hayek's Principal Writings
Published in English

Prices and Production, Routledge & Kegan Paul, 1931.

Monetary Theory and the Trade Cycle, Jonathan Cape, 1933.

Monetary Nationalism and International Stability, Longmans, 1937.

Profits, Interest and Investment, Routledge & Kegan Paul, 1939.

The Pure Theory of Capital, Routledge & Kegan Paul, 1941.

The Road to Serfdom, 1944.*

Individualism and Economic Order, 1948 (Germany 1952).*

John Stuart Mill and Harriet Taylor, 1951.*

The Sensory Order, 1952.*

The Counter-Revolution of Science, The Free Press, Glencoe, Ill., 1955.

The Political Ideal of the Rule of Law, Cairo, 1955.

The Constitution of Liberty, 1960.*

Studies in Philosophy, Politics and Economics, 1967.*

Law, Legislation and Liberty, Vol. I: *Rules and Order*, 1973.*

* Published by Routledge & Kegan Paul, London, and University of Chicago Press, Chicago, Ill.

A Short Note on
Austrian Capital Theory

*At a late stage Miss Sudha Shenoy, who compiled and intro-
duced the extracts in* A Tiger *by the Tail, was asked to
write a thumbnail sketch of Austrian capital theory for
readers to whom it was unfamiliar, and to indicate texts
where they could study it at more length.*—ED.

AUSTRIAN CAPITAL theory views capital not as a homogeneous
stock but as a network of interrelated goods: a diversified structure
of complementary elements, rather than a uniform lump. The
process of production is seen as occurring in a series of 'stages',
extending from final consumption to stages successively further
removed. To take a simple example: a steel mill *by itself* cannot
produce final consumption goods, such as cars or washing
machines. In order to produce such consumer goods, a whole
intervening chain of complementary investments is required – in
factories, machinery, stocks of raw materials, etc. The steel mill's
output passes into the next stage of production as an input,
together with other inputs (raw materials, etc.), and is used in the
factories in this stage to produce various intermediate goods.
These goods in turn serve as inputs for the next stage of production, until final consumption is reached.

Thus, investments in wholesale and retail distribution, in this
view, are complementary to investments in previous stages of
production; they are an integral part of the capital structure as
a whole necessary to bring goods to the final consumption stage.
Particular capital goods may be specific to one stage of production; or they may be adaptable to several stages.

In other words, a miscellaneous jumble of non-consumption
goods will *not necessarily* raise final output. Individual capital
investments (whether in plant, machinery, raw materials or semi-
finished goods) must fit into an integrated capital structure,
completed to the final consumption stage, if they are to add to

final consumption output. Investments that do not form such an integrated structure are (or become) *mal*-investments yielding capital and operating losses.

The 'filigree' (i.e. composition) of capital goods forming a co-ordinated capital structure changes with circumstances. Thus a factory, once profitable, becomes unprofitable as the circumstances in which it was originally built are themselves altered. Equally, new investment opportunities open up with changing circumstances; investments once useless may become profitable again. In short, capital is *not* automatically maintained intact; neither is any investment automatically profitable in all circumstances.

The essential role of prices (and of rates of return on individual goods) emerges from this brief outline. Only if there exist markets in which prices reflect (changing) relative scarcities of the different sorts of capital goods involved can the capital structure as a whole be integrated, and mal-investments be revealed.

May 1975   SUDHA SHENOY

Sources

Hayek, F. A., *Prices and Production*, 2nd Edn., 1933, Lectures 2 & 3 and Appendix: 'Capital and Industrial Fluctuations'.
A Tiger by the Tail, compiled by Sudha Shenoy, Hobart Paperback 4, Institute of Economic Affairs, 1972.

Kirzner, Israel, *An Essay on Capital*, Augustus M. Kelley, New York, 1966.

Lachmann, L. M., *Capital and Its Structure*, Bell, London, 1956.

Mises, Ludwig von, *Human Action*, Wm. Hodge, Edinburgh, 1949, *passim*.

Rothbard, Murray N., *Man, Economy and State*, Chs. 5, 6, 7 (Vol. I) and 8 (Vol. II), Nash Publications, Los Angeles, 1970.